Seven

Worship

Words

Meditating on Jesus

Michael Holsten

Dedication

This book is dedicated to You, Jesus. Thank You for making it a blessing to me. Please make it a blessing to all who read it.

Acknowledgement

Thanks to my wife, Rita, for her careful editing of this work. You have greatly improved this small book which I offer for the Lord's use.

Contents

Preface

Christ, Jesus, Savior, Lord, praise to You.

These words of worship have been inspiring and full of meaning to me. I pray that after reading this, you will be blessed in using them, too.

The first part of this booklet opens each word to look at the meaning from the Bible, the way God's people used the word, and the way we can use the word for worship.

The second part is a collection of suggestions for how to use these words. I hope you will browse through these suggestions and let the Lord show you those that will be helpful and meaningful in your worship life.

Worship is not something perfect people do in a perfect church building, speaking perfect words, wearing perfect clothes, singing perfect hymns, perfectly in tune, always perfectly understanding and applying God's Word perfectly. For me, worship is a privilege that happens in church, but also along the way each day (hence the cover picture).

These seven worship words are packed full of joy and power and life. They are not a magic mantra. Repeating them over and over will not perform miracles or change life. On the other hand, using them in worship in a regular way, will, I believe, draw you closer to Jesus, to His gracious will, and to His power for your life. And if He does perform miracles and change our lives, that's ok, too.

The tempter tries to take the joy and power out of our worship. He tries to get us to just say words with our mouths, without our head or heart or spirit participating. It requires prayerful discipline to approach every worship time in a way that keeps us from being distracted or self-centered. The chapter on the word "You" has a discussion that is in this context.

I pray that you will find suggestions in the second part of the book that will be effective for you in keeping your focus on Jesus as you use these words.

Worship is sometimes a solemn, possibly quiet event. But sometimes it is more than that. I have discovered, and I hope you have, too, that our gracious Lord is with us always. That means that the words of Solomon in Ecclesiastes 2.25 apply to us now: "For who can eat and who can have enjoyment without Him?" Since Paul tells us to "Rejoice always" (Phil 4.4), we can worship and rejoice also when we are doing mundane things at home or work, and when we are having times of recreation and enjoyment. (The Lord is the expert at "re-creation".)

By suggesting that we can worship the Lord every day in the small and large things we do, I hope I am clear that this is not instead of worship together with other Christians every week in church. Worship together in the body of Christ is where the Lord has promised to meet us ("For where two or three have gathered together in My name, I am there in their midst." Matt. 18.20). That is the essential place for us to receive the Lord's mercy and grace, and celebrate His gracious gifts together. (Heb. 10.25)

When we speak the seven words described in this booklet, we are speaking to Jesus, directly, personally, in that place, at that specific moment in time. And He is with us. He is, of course, always with us, but when we speak in this way to Him, we *know* that He is there with us in that place, at that very moment. We recognize Him with us. These words, I believe, help us to be aware that we are living with Him and by His grace in the moments of our speaking.

So during your day, at any time, you can speak with these words to Jesus and know that He is there listening to you, with you, loving you, encouraging you, even helping you have enjoyment. I hope recognizing Jesus with you, and the Father with Whom He is One, and the Spirit who proceeds from Them, will open you to new joy and to living with faith, wonder, awe, and closeness to our Lord in your life.

May you live with Jesus, talk to Jesus, and listen to Jesus. May you worship Jesus our Savior, our Father Who loves us, and the Spirit, Who gives us His power to live. And may worship be a part of your life every day.

Michael Holsten

Christ

"Aunt Stella will be here in two weeks!" Good news? If you are greatly looking forward to seeing Aunt Stella again, then it is good news. For children the promised coming of a wonderful (translate: treats them like people and is willing to listen to them) aunt may be great good news. It may be difficult for the children to wait for Aunt Stella to come. The days will seem to go by very slowly.

After God promised the coming of the Messiah to Adam and Eve, people had to wait for what seemed a very long time.

The promise is given first in Gen. 3.15:
"And I will put enmity
between you and the woman,
and between your seed and her seed;
He shall bruise you on the head,
and you shall bruise him on the heel."

Is He here yet? When is He coming? Why do we have to wait? What is He going to say? What is He going to do? What will we do when He comes?

With the fervor of a four-year-old in the back seat, the questions just kept coming. For all the years of the Old Testament, people waited with questions bubbling up. There had been a promise. (Gen 3.15) Eve might have been thinking of the promise's fulfillment when she had her first child. (Gen 4.1) Generation after generation, people waited for Messiah to come.

And then He came, and the Greek word used by the writers of the New Testament for Messiah translates as Christ.

In order for Christ to be the Promised One, Someone has to do the promising. Christ is very clear Who that is. In the gospel of John alone, Christ refers to "the One Who sent Me" 24 times. So when we use the word "Christ" we have the opportunity to remember our gracious Father. We don't worship Christ in isolation from God our Father. When we meditate on Christ, as the One Who was sent, we also meditate on our Father who loved us so much that He sent … the Messiah … His Son … Christ.

With the word "Christ", we worship the One who is the fulfillment of the promise God gave in the Garden of Eden. We worship the One awaited by all God's people throughout the Old Testament. With the title "Christ", we let the enthusiasm of the "four-year-old in the backseat" explode in our hearts with a resounding "Yes!" while celebrating that He has come, with feelings of joy, thanksgiving, wonder, and awe.

The Greek word "Christ" also has the meaning of the Anointed One. People were anointed in Old Testament times to enter a particular service or ministry. David was anointed to be king. (1 Samuel 16.13) Elisha was anointed to be a prophet. (1 Kings 19.16) With the word "Christ", we remember that Jesus was also anointed by God:

Peter tells Cornelius in Acts 10.38: "You know of Jesus of Nazareth, how God anointed Him with the Holy Spirit and with power, and how He went about doing good and healing all who were oppressed by the devil, for God was with Him."

So when we worship using the word "Christ", our hearts overflow with thanksgiving because of the promise given by our Father, the Promiser, because of the fulfillment of His promise, and because of the anointing our Father gave Christ to carry out His mission for us.

Jesus

"What's his name?" THE question parents are asked when people see their infant son for the first time. A person needs a name in order for us to consider a child to be a real person. How would you feel meeting friends with their newborn son if they had not yet chosen a name for him? It might seem like a time of waiting. It might seem like the person had not yet completely arrived.

God the Father provided the name for His Son. The angel Gabriel knew Jesus' name before He was conceived (Luke 2.21). The angel told Mary the name her son was to receive (Luke 1.31). An angel appeared to Joseph in a dream and told him what name to give his son. The angel also explained to Joseph the reason for using this name (Matt. 1.21), "for He will save His people from their sins."

So Jesus got His name and it meant a lot to people then and to us now, because the Christ, promised of old was no longer just Messiah, but a Person named Jesus. When we worship Jesus, we are not thinking of a name in a history book. We are not thinking of a picture. We are not thinking of a story we have heard. We are thinking of a Person.

Jesus enjoyed Mary's cooking. (Maybe Joseph's, possibly His grandmother's.) He went through the education for boys. Jesus was a person who did a lot of walking (the car, the bus, and for that matter, the paved road being quite a ways off). He was invited to weddings. He got tired and slept, even in moving boats. He participated in Synagogue services. He had family gatherings with relatives (who didn't think much of Him). He didn't watch TV or read mysteries, but he liked people and was a good listener.

Jesus' Father was God. He didn't sin. He really did live at a particular place and time on this planet. So, when we meditate on Jesus, we can think of a person that we can shake hands with.

At the same time, the Person we worship is unique because he was a Person before He was conceived (John 8.58). He was there at creation (John 1.1 – 3, Gen 1.26). He appears in other places in the Old Testament. In Gen 11.7 He is mentioned at the Tower of Babel.

Christ has come—and He is the person, Jesus. What, then, does He have to do with us?

Savior

Paul wrote to Titus: "Grace and peace from God our Father and Christ Jesus our Savior." (Titus 1.4)

Jesus, the One we worship, is the Christ, and He is also our Savior. "How great is that! I have a Savior! So, Jesus, I'll let You know when I need Your help." Not exactly. Jesus is Savior *because* we need one, not if and when we need one.

When God promised the Messiah to come, it was because Adam and Eve had left the perfection in which God created them. They had decided they knew better than God and had disobeyed him. (Gen. 3.1-13) They were no longer perfect. They were sinners. All those who are descended from them (including us) are also sinners. (Rom 3.23)

If we still think we are perfect, there is surely a wife, husband, friend, father, mother, son or daughter who will straighten us out on this subject. But we don't just need a Savior because we sin. David made it clear, "in sin my mother conceived me." (Psalm 51.5) He is not saying that conceiving children is a sin, but that when a child is conceived that child is a sinner from conception because he is a descendent of Adam and Eve who sinned.

So we don't have to wait until something terrible happens to need a Savior. We are sinners now! We deserve to be condemned by God now! We need a Savior now!

Good News! Jesus, the Christ who has come, is that Savior.

So Jesus came and touched people or told them they were saved, and that was it, right? Nope. 1 John 1.7 says, "...the blood of Jesus His Son cleanses us from all sin." We are saved because we are cleansed by the blood of Jesus, not because He is divine, which He is. Rather, we are saved because Jesus sacrificed Himself on the cross for us.

Paul in Col. 2.13,14 describes God forgiving our sins and making us alive with Christ by taking our debt of sin and nailing it to the cross. Jesus gave His life for us, suffering, not just physical death, but eternal punishment for our sins, shedding His blood for us on the cross. (Matt. 27.46: "My God, My God, why have You forsaken Me?") It cost God a lot for us to be forgiven.

Now we are forgiven, we have a Savior, and we are saved. (Acts 15.11) Because we have been set free *from* our sin, we are made alive with Jesus forever. We have been set free *for* a new life, a life where we rejoice to have Jesus be our Savior. What does that new life look like?

Lord

What if He came to you and told you...

...to pack up and move to another city where He will have instructions for what you are to do?

...to stop doing what you are doing, go back to school, and trust Him as you start a new career?

...to go to someone you know and He would tell you what to say when you get there?

...to tell the first person you see after you leave home today that Jesus loves them?

Who is He to tell me something like that?

That was the question the Pharisees had with Jesus. "By what authority..." (Matt. 21.23) They had a good thing going, and here comes this country preacher telling people to change their attitudes, their lives, and their worship.

The One we recognize as Lord is the One who has the right to tell us anything and expect our obedience. If He is Lord, He is the One we can depend on, no matter what.

We are servants of Him, the One who is Lord. The word that Paul uses for servant means slave. Our relationship to Jesus is that He is in complete charge of where we are, what we do, how we live, what we have, what we say—He is in complete charge of our entire life.

For people who value having an independent spirit, that can be scary. People can be heard talking about, "my life, my plans, my property, my possessions, my job, my weekend, my time, ..." The idea that everything we have, our health, all our time, our future here and in eternity—all of it comes from the Lord, belongs to Him and is graciously given according to His will—this is an idea that is threatening unless Jesus is the Christ and our Savior.

Jesus, Who is all-powerful, can be threatening until we know how much He loves us and until we receive the great blessing that He becomes our personal Savior. Because He loves us, we receive power from Him so that we can begin loving Him.

Then it is wonderful that He is really, actually, right now, our Lord—always, everywhere, no matter what happens to us.

It took a lot for the disciples to call Jesus Lord with all their hearts and being. It took the cross.

It took the Resurrection. They knew He was really Somebody. They knew God the Father claimed Him as His Son. Some had seen Him transfigured with glory, that showed heaven shining through Him. However, they had seen Him die—on a cross. They needed something pretty amazing to be Jesus' witnesses to us. Then, He came through the locked doors of the upper room on Easter evening. He had appeared to the women in the morning, but the disciples had trouble shifting gears that quickly. Now they were jerked into the new reality—Jesus was alive, permanently. He not only had authority and power. He not only loved recklessly. He was their living, loving, in charge now and forever, Lord.

Then at Pentecost, with the gift of the Holy Spirit, the disciples were set free and empowered to proclaim Him eternal, wonderful, gracious Lord, to all people, for all time—with their words, with their writing, with their lives, with their death—to proclaim Him Lord, even to us, now. (John 17.17-21)

It is only by the Holy Spirit that we can, without fear, with love and worship, call Jesus our Lord with all our being. ("Therefore I make known to you that no one speaking by the Spirit of God says, 'Jesus is accursed'; and no one can say, 'Jesus is Lord,' except by the Holy Spirit." 1 Cor. 12.3) When we worship using the word "Lord", we include the Holy Spirit in our worship. It is only by the Holy Spirit that we worship Jesus as absolute Lord of our life.

If Christ Jesus, our Savior, is our Lord, how do we fit Him into our life? Paste Him onto our Sunday mornings (some Sundays? Most Sundays?)? The Spirit shows us quickly that our Lord does not "fit" into our life. We live in Him ("for in Him we live and move and exist, as even some of your own poets have said, 'For we also are His children.'" Acts 17.28).

Can you imagine, after our Lord was welcomed back to heaven in a ceremony vastly more glorious than the terrific scene at the end of Star Wars, we would then say, "I have a few moments for You on Tuesday afternoon at 4 p.m., if that's ok, Lord?"

The reality is that we have been blessed beyond our wildest dreams. Our Lord graciously fits us into *His* Life. So now, we have a new and wonderful privilege.

Praise

What do you say if the President comes to visit? Are we so brash as to say, "Hello, Mr. President. Thank you for coming. I have some suggestions on how to run the country that I know you have been looking forward to hearing ." Do we treat God the same way?

When God speaks to us in His word, we see something very different. The recurring theme in Scripture is wonder and awe, thanksgiving and honor, coming from people's hearts when they say, "Praise!"

Praise is not something thought of by people which God kind of likes. It is His idea: "The Lord heard my cry...He put a new song in my mouth, A song of praise to our God." (Ps 40.1-3)

As God's people, we ask God to help us talk to Him with praise: "O Lord, open my lips, that my mouth may declare Your praise." (Ps 51.15)

What are we doing when we praise God? We are recognizing who God is. We are recognizing God is gracious and loves us without our deserving it. We are worshiping our gracious God, Father, Son, and Holy Spirit. We are thanking God for Who He is and for what He has done for us and for what He has given us. (Ps 63.3 "Because Your lovingkindness is better than life, my lips will praise You.")

And who is to praise God? Jesus shows us praising by his own words of praising for His Father. (Matt. 11.25: "At that time Jesus said, 'I praise You, Father, Lord of heaven and earth, that You have hidden these things from *the* wise and intelligent and have revealed them to infants.'") It is God's intention for all people to praise Him. (Ps 67.3 "Let the peoples praise You, O God; Let all the peoples praise You.") We want future generations to also praise God. (Ps 102.18: "This will be written for the generation to come, that a people yet to be created may praise the LORD.") When we praise God we can appreciate the fellowship we have with the angels who are also praising God. (Psalm 148.2: "Praise Him, all His angels.")

So when are people (like us) to praise God? It may be on our schedule to praise God when we rise in the morning and at the end of the day.

The Lord's schedule is, however, different. He speaks to us in terms of "continually" and "all day long". (Ps 34.1 "I will bless the Lord at all times, His praise shall continually be in my mouth.") (Ps 71.8 "My mouth is filled with Your praise, And with Your glory all day long.")

There are also some particular times to praise. Praise, the Lord tells us, when our spirit is faint with discouragement or mourning. (Isaiah 61.1-3: "The Spirit of the Lord God is upon me...To grant those who mourn in Zion...The mantle of praise instead of a spirit of fainting.") Praise also in adversity, when we feel under attack. (Acts 16.25: "But about midnight Paul and Silas were praying and singing hymns of praise to God, and the prisoners were listening to them.")

Of course, we are not the first to hear these encouragements to praise. God's people for millennia have been praising God in writing, in prayers, in conversation, in song, in living. Before Jesus was born, God's people praised the Lord. Since Jesus came and lived among people, they have praised the Lord.

When you stand near train tracks, you can hear a train coming, going by, and going on to its destination. Imagine that you are hearing the train of praise to our gracious God coming from the past, coming close to you. (Psalm 111.10: "His praise endures forever.") Imagine that you get to add your praise during your life to that train of praise. Then the train keeps going on into the future for more of God's people to include their praise. That train is close to us now and we get to participate in the joy that is eternal by adding our praises.

We praise Jesus as we talk to Him in these seven words. But more than that, we also praise our Father, because He is the One who promised the Messiah. When we say, "Christ", we recognize not only the One promised, but also the One who did the promising. And when we say, "Savior", we recognize not only Jesus who has saved us by giving Himself into death to give us Life, we also recognize the Spirit Who is the only One Who brings the good news of our Savior to us, personally. The Spirit is the One Who effectively brings us to Life. By grace, we are saved through faith, and the Holy Spirit gives us that faith so that we can recognize Jesus as our Savior. (Eph. 2.8) So we include the Holy Spirit in our praise when we say, "Savior".

Let us then, with the Spirit leading us and encouraging us, praise the Lord with our lips and all our being, increasingly through our days. (Dancing and music encouraged.) (Ps 71.14: "But as for me, I will hope continually, and will praise You yet more and more.") (Isaiah 12.5 "Praise the LORD in song, for He has done excellent things; let this be known throughout the earth.") (Ps 149.3 "Let them praise His name with dancing; Let them sing praises to Him with timbrel and lyre.") (Eph. 1.12 "...to the end that we who were the first to hope in Christ would be to the praise of His glory.")

To

When we say, "Praise to You," what is the "to" doing there? There is the praise. It is in the hearts of God's people for ages. It is in our hearts. There is Jesus. The "to" is the pipeline, the connection between the "praise" and "You." It is our *personal* connection.

We are doing the praising. We are sending praise to Jesus with our heart. In the seven words, the word "to" makes it personal.

We can read about God's people in the past praising God. We are thinking about praise, we may be learning about praise. But we are not praising. We can read words in worship that include words of praise. Our eyes see the words and perhaps our lips speak them. Probably, you have enough experience to know that this can happen without the process involving your heart.

When the Holy Spirit lets us know The Christ, the person Jesus, our Savior and our Lord with faith in our hearts, He sets our very being on fire so that we *want* praise to come from *us.* We don't want to just see the words or read the words of praise. We want them to be *our* words. We want to be involved in the praise process. We want to participate in the eternal event of praising God our Father, our Savior, the Spirit of Life.

"To" is us. This is our heart sending the message to Jesus. This is our stamp on the envelope. This is our push of the button to send email or text. This is the breath of our spirit on Skype or FaceTime. This is the expression of love and joy and thanksgiving and wonder and awe on our face as we speak to our Savior who is in the room with us. "To" is our own personal reaching out to touch and honor and love Jesus, Himself, personally--to touch the "You" Who is with us where we are.

You

There was a time...   When you could write a letter and get an answer in three or four months, depending on weather, pony express, or ship schedules. When you could write a letter and get an answer in a couple of weeks, depending on Post Office holidays or weekends involved. When you could call a person and speak in real time and get an immediate answer. When you can email. When you can text. When you can Skype or FaceTime. When you can walk into the next room and be with a person to whom you are talking.

What difference does it make? In a negative sense, there is the teacher who says to a student, "Would you say that, if your mother were here?" (I have had good and some very bad results with that.) It is possible that the mother's presence would change the behavior of a student. In a positive sense, are there people you know whose smile and personal joy are so infectious that when you are in their presence, your conversation and thinking become more positive and hopeful?

Conversing with Jesus by reading a prayer might be meaningful. Perhaps it would be more meaningful if we are talking in a conversational tone in prayer from our heart. However, the most meaningful of all is if Jesus is in the room with us. Can you imagine talking to Jesus without distractions of family, television, radio, extraneous thoughts, or "wool-gathering"? Can you imagine talking to Jesus, being in the same room with Him, with Him looking at you and an expression of love on His face as He is intently listening to you?!

The "You" in "Christ Jesus, Savior, Lord, praise to You" is that kind of experience. All that we treasure in our heart about Jesus being the Christ, promised by our Father, about Jesus being a particular

Person Who was born some time ago, about Jesus being our Savior according to God's plan, about Jesus being the very Lord of our life now and forever, about the joy and worship we express in praise to Him, about that praise coming from us personally, right now—all that we treasure in our heart, we are speaking from our heart to Him, now, in the same room with us, or to Him outside, wherever we are, looking at us, listening to us, loving us.

We are talking to Him, we know He is listening, and we are expecting Him to hear us—our words, our heart, our praise, our joy. Unless He graciously lets us see Him before we die, besides the blessings of His sacraments, this is as close as we can get to Him until we see Him at home—in the home He has graciously prepared for us.

What a joy and privilege we have to speak to Jesus, here and now. We are not just sending a message to be delivered at some future time at some distant place, wherever Jesus is. We are participating in an eternal line of servants of Jesus speaking praise to Him, but for us, it is right here and right now, and He is right here with us, listening to us and loving us.

Our time, our plans, our thoughts, our desires are turned over to Him to see, to change, to bless as we praise Him. Our day is connected to Him in joy and expectation, with wonder that we get to live with Jesus, and with confidence that Jesus is with us in this day that He has given to us.

Thank you, Christ, Jesus, Savior, Lord that You are with us here, now, listening to us, receiving our praise, loving us, speaking Your love and guidance to us with Your heart. Thank You that we may live in this day, for You and with You. We pray in confidence in You and in Your grace. Amen.

PART 2

I believe the goal in talking to the Lord is to have our whole heart and mind focused on talking to Him and listening to Him. What connections can we make in worship that will make the worship experience more real and satisfying? This part 2 has suggestions on how to do that.

Did Adam and Eve have garage sales? I don't know, but I suppose it is possible. Whether it is a garage sale, spending a day at the mall, looking for treasures at Goodwill (one of my wife's and my favorites), or surfing Amazon, it is possible to sort through a lot of things to find something that you really like and find useful. That is what I invite you to do in this second part.

After you have used the seven words in talking to the Lord, I invite you to look through these suggestions and find those that will be a blessing to you.

1 When?

When is a good time to use these seven words in conversing with the Lord?

a. If you have a time for exercise regularly, you might use these seven words then. Once you have the routine of exercise down, it can be pretty boring, even if you know you are doing something really wonderful for your body. Exercise machines might have music or TV available. However, using the time for conversation with the Lord can make it an exercise of the spirit as well as the body. When your body is wide awake and in motion, it is possible for your spirit to have a wide awake, satisfying time with the Lord.

b. Certainly, the beginning of the day is a good time to set the day in a direction of being aware of the Lord's presence by taking time for focused worship.

c. You might use these words to enter into a personal worship time when you go to church.

d. While, for most people, life seems to move at a fast pace, there seem to be times when we are waiting for something. Waiting for the children to get ready (or the spouse?). Waiting for the bus or train. Waiting to get where you are going. [Disclaimer: As with phones, not getting in the way of driving, right?] At the checkout line, at the bank, at school. If the game or movie has a particularly slow time. Waiting for the food to come or be ready. These are times when we can talk to the Lord and worship.

e. Sometimes we start a task with enthusiasm, sometimes with resignation, and sometimes with absolute dread. In any case, we can begin our task talking to the Lord and entrusting what we do to Him. In these words, we can be honest when we are starting something we are not looking forward to. By praising Jesus, we can ask Him to give us the attitude, insight, ability, enjoyment, strength, and endurance we need.

f. Then there are times when we are staring into space and find ourselves confused about what is, after all, actually happening. This can be an excellent time to touch base with Him, Who is our Rock in every day, in every need.

g. There are times when we are physically not feeling good, feeling lousy, or actually suffering. We want Jesus to be close to us. We want to know that we are still in His care. We can reach out to Him with these words to experience His presence to help us get through.

h. When darkness attacks our mind or heart, we can feel like evil is in the room with us. It might be fears, worries, or memories of past events that are attacking. When we start saying these worship words it might be that—just saying them. However, we can keep it up until we know we are talking to Jesus in the room with us, pushing out all darkness with the light of His presence.

2 How?

How can we use these words? What are some different ways?

a. Most commonly, we might use these words to speak in prayer. We can speak out loud because we talk to other people that way and it's ok to talk to Jesus out loud. Sometimes talking out loud is the only way to be louder than other voices in our head or heart.

b. Then, there are times when we want to whisper as we use these words. When we are focusing on whispering, perhaps we are more focused about this being a special time and an important communication.

c. Sometimes, it is helpful or appropriate to silently think these words as we converse with the Lord. We can be thinking them when there is something going on around us in which we want the Lord's presence. We might think them to keep our sanity when the "noise" around us seems to be coming from evil and not from the Lord.

d. Sing! "O come, let us sing for joy to the Lord." (Ps 95.1) Make up your own music. Use a tune you like. [Some hymn tunes you might like are on http://www.hymntime.com/tch/mid/met/10.10%20D.htm and some to try are #9, 26, 31, 54, 55, 58, 76, 83, and 90] Sing these words. Put power, emotion, joy, wonder, love, and enthusiasm in them. Sing! (Puff, the Magic Dragon?)

e. Use these words with silent times interspersed for listening to the Lord. Use all seven a couple times, then wait with Samuel's attitude, "Speak Lord, for your servant is listening." (1 Samuel 3.10).

f. You might try using different speeds when you use these words. When you vary the speed, it might help you concentrate on what you are saying. For example, fast, slow, fast, medium, slow, fast.

g. You might try using the relationship of the words to each other: The seven words are not independent. Consider using these seven words in prayer or worship while considering the relationship of each of the words to "Christ," Who was sent by our Father. Then, use them considering the relationship of each to "Jesus." a Person Who understands us. Then, in relation to "Savior," Who has rescued us by His sacrifice. Then, in relation to "Lord," Who is truly God and King of the world. Again, in relation to "Praise" considering our God-given privilege and purpose. Again, in relation to the word "To" that involves us by His wonderful grace. Last in relation to "You" with which we tie each worship word to the One with us at that very moment.

h. You might use these worship words connecting them to seasons in the Church Year. "Christ" has to do with the season of Advent (the three or four weeks before Christmas). During this season, the focus is on the promise of God to send the Messiah, the Christ, and how the fulfillment is coming at Jesus' birth and at His second coming. "Jesus" has to do with Christmas (and Epiphany) when the focus is on God coming as true man, a real person. "Savior" connects to Lent, the season showing Jesus sacrificing Himself for us on the cross, to forgive us our sins and to give us Life in Him. "Lord" has to do with the recognition of Jesus as the Risen One, God, the Lord in the Easter season. "Praise", to me, has to do with the Pentecost season. It is the Holy Spirit Who calls us to the fulfilling purpose of praising our Lord and shows us in the life of Jesus how we may apply His word to living lives of praise. "To" connects to our coming to faith in Jesus at the day of our baptism or some other date or time. "You" connects to Today, the day you are using these words to worship the Lord.

i. Another way to vary your use of these words is to use different languages that you might know. A Latin translation might be "Christus, Iesus, Salvator et Dominus, laudate tibi." Spanish might be "Cristo, Jesús, Salvador, Señor, gloria a ti." German: "Christus, Jesus, Retter, Herr, Lob an Sie." Others can be created on https://translate.google.com/#en/

j. There are times when music in the background helps us focus our worship. You might try chant or hymn music.

k. You can use a Bible passage of your choice to help focus your worship/prayer/conversation time. (See section 3 "Using a Bible Passage")

l. You might use one of the names of Jesus to help focus. (See section 4 "Connect to a Name of Jesus")

m. Another way to focus is to think of a picture while you are using these words. (See section 5 "Use a Picture")

n. Using a Bible story is also a way to focus (See section 6 "Use a Bible Story")

o. The last section in Part 2 is section 7 "Further Study," where you can review and study more Scripture references for each of the seven worship words.

3 Using a Bible Passage

When you pray or worship using these seven words you can use a Bible passage to focus your heart. Here are some examples.

A favorite passage of mine is John 14.27:

[27] Peace I leave with you; My peace I give to you; not as the world gives do I give to you. Do not let your heart be troubled, nor let it be fearful.

Where would we be without "Christ" being sent according to promise—without peace. "Jesus", the person, cared about His disciples and us by saying these words. The peace that is His, that lets us not be afraid comes to us because He is our "Savior". We want to follow our "Lord," who gives us peace and wants us to live without fear. "Praise" is our natural response to His love—His coming and providing life in His peace. "To" involves us receiving that peace and enjoying it daily, as we depend on the One Who is with us, the One Who is "You" that we talk to.

Another longer favorite is Psalm 121:

I will lift up my eyes to the mountains;
From where shall my help come?
[2] My help comes from the LORD,
Who made heaven and earth.
[3] He will not allow your foot to slip;
He who keeps you will not slumber.
[4] Behold, He who keeps Israel
Will neither slumber nor sleep.

5 The LORD is your keeper;
The LORD is your shade on your right hand.
6 The sun will not smite you by day,
Nor the moon by night.
7 The LORD will protect you from all evil;
He will keep your soul.
8 The LORD will guard your going out and your coming in
From this time forth and forever.

There is some difference between the use of the word "Lord" (in small capitals) in the Old Testament and the word "Lord" (not in small capitals) in the New Testament. In the Old Testament, the word refers to Yahweh, the name of God. In the New Testament, the word generally refers to God, to Jesus, and to the quality of lordship that Jesus possesses graciously toward us. (See the first part on "Lord".)

Our help comes from the Lord. In "Christ" we remember God's promise to give us THE help we need by sending the Messiah to restore us in our eternal relationship with Him. The psalmist speaks of the One who is helping us as a person as we also consider "Jesus" a real person. Keeping our soul and guarding us now and forever surely is Jesus being our "Savior". When we look for help, we look to the One Who is our "Lord", Whom we depend on and follow, now and forever. As we read this psalm and remember how God loves us and how He takes care of us, "Praise" comes naturally from our heart. We want it directed from us personally, "To" our Lord personally, ("You").

It is probably possible to take any Bible passage and find connections to the seven words. The qualities of a focus passage that are most helpful, however, are that the passage is meaningful to you, has to do with God's love for us, shows us or describes God's grace in Jesus, has to do with God's promises, has to do with prayer, or makes us feel that we are in Jesus' presence.

If you are reading through the Bible in some plan, you might be on the lookout, as you read, for a verse that touches you in one of those ways. Then, as you use that verse or those verses, you can have a conversation using the seven words, thinking about the passage, with our Lord. You can listen to Him, to see what He has to say to you to encourage you, strengthen you, or guide you.

It might be a good idea to have a way to record what the Lord gives you in a journal of some kind, a book, an electronic file, a smart phone list. As you look back over the years, the conversations take on new and lasting meaning.

Here are some more Bible passages to consider:

Deut 31.8 "The Lord is the one who goes ahead of you; He will be with you. He will not fail you or forsake you. Do not fear or be dismayed."

Deut 33.27 "The eternal God is a dwelling place,
And underneath are the everlasting arms."

Neh 8.10 "Do not be grieved, for the joy of the Lord is your strength."

Ps 27.13, 14 "I would have despaired unless I had believed that I would see the goodness of the Lord in the land of the living. Wait for the Lord; be strong and let your heart take courage; Yes, wait for the Lord."

Ps 116.8,9 "For You have rescued my soul from death,
My eyes from tears,
My feet from stumbling.
I shall walk before the Lord
In the land of the living."

Is 40.31 "Yet those who wait for the Lord
Will gain new strength;
They will mount up with wings like eagles,
They will run and not get tired,
They will walk and not become weary."

Matt 11.28,29 "Come to Me, all who are weary and heavy-laden, and I will give you rest. Take My yoke upon you and learn from Me, for I am gentle and humble in heart, and you will find rest for your souls."

Rom 15.13 "Now may the God of hope fill you with all joy and peace in believing, so that you will abound in hope by the power of the Holy Spirit."

2 Cor 5.15 "...and He died for all, so that they who live might no longer live for themselves, but for Him who died and rose again on their behalf."

Phil 4.7 "And the peace of God, which surpasses all comprehension, will guard your hearts and your minds in Christ Jesus."

Col 3.15-17 "Let the peace of Christ rule in your hearts, to which indeed you were called in one body; and be thankful. Let the word of Christ richly dwell within you, with all wisdom teaching and admonishing one another with psalms and hymns and spiritual songs, singing with thankfulness in your hearts to God. Whatever you do in word or deed, do all in the name of the Lord Jesus, giving thanks through Him to God the Father."

2 Tim 1.7 "For God has not given us a spirit of timidity, but of power and love and discipline."

1 Peter 5.7 "...casting all your anxiety on Him, because He cares for you."

Rev 22.20 "He who testifies to these things says, 'Yes, I am coming quickly.' Amen. Come, Lord Jesus."

4 Connect to a Name of Jesus

Some names of Jesus:

Jesus is the "Word of God".

In the beginning was the Word, and the Word was with God, and the Word was God. John 1.1

God speaks His Word to us, as Christ, the Light coming into the world (John 1.9), as Jesus, the Word become flesh (John 1.14), as Savior, Who gave the right to become children of God (John 1.12), as Lord, the Word with glory as the only begotten from the Father (John 1.14), as the One Who lights up all darkness and gives us reason to praise Him (John 1.5), as the One Who touches us (we come into being only through Him, John 1.3) and brings praise from us To the Word Himself Who gives us "grace upon grace" (John 1.16).

Jesus is the "Bright Morning Star".

I am the root and the descendant of David, the bright morning star. Rev. 22.16

He is the star that is so bright He shines to us, in us, through us, day and night. He is the Morning Star, the beginning of the day that never ends in darkness. He is Christ, the One sent to break open the world to let in Starlight. He is Jesus, the Person we can relate to, who shows us Starlight. He is Savior, the Starlight in action lighting up our lives. He is Lord, Starlight shining on us and through us opening the darkness ahead of us. Praise is due Him who Lights up our life. We rejoice that we may speak praise with our hearts To Him, Morning Star with us throughout each day. We speak to "You", the One Who is with us, with confidence that His brightness always grows for us through time.

If focusing on a name of Jesus is helpful to you, here are some suggested websites that give other names of Jesus:

http://bibleresources.org/names-of-jesus/

http://www.biblegateway.com/resources/dictionary-of-bible-themes/2203-Jesus-Christ-titles-names

http://www.gotquestions.org/names-Jesus-Christ.html

5 Use a Picture

There is a picture in my mind (which I have as a photograph somewhere) of a spot on a trail in New Mexico. In one direction, down into the valley is a small city. In the opposite direction, uphill, the trail goes between weathered tall outcroppings that go up to the top of the small mountain chain.

Perhaps you have similar pictures that you can bring to mind. What happens if you use these seven words and imagine yourself talking to Jesus in that picture, in that place.

In my picture, I feel my praise directed to Jesus for creating such a beautiful, inspiring, satisfying place where I can feel myself walking with Him. I can sense His enjoyment of His creation. I can sense His caring about the many people who live in the valley who, tragically, have not enjoyed His peace. It seems that my small praise echoes off the mountain and reaches down into the valley, flitting between the many noises there, trying to draw the attention of people to the One Who loves them and Who made the mountains they might take for granted. The sunshine in my picture grows brighter, and there is a song celebrating the promise, the Person, the rescuing, the Lordship, the rightful praise for God's creation and grace, a song that lifts my spirit and lets me see Jesus smiling.

Whether it is a picture of a place, a picture in your mind, a painting you have seen, or a remembered event, you might consider holding that image in your mind and heart while you say these seven words and look for what Jesus does with that picture for you.

One particular way to use this experience is to consider a picture or memory about which you feel grief, sorrow, guilt, or embarrassment. As you speak these seven words, allow Jesus to bring the picture or memory into different focus, with different feelings that bring healing for you. How has the situation changed? How have relationships changed? (Reference: *The Gift of Inner Healing* by Ruth Carter Stapleton).

You might also use a picture that brings great joy to you. One picture that does that for me is "A Room With A View" by Thomas Kinkade. [https://thomaskinkade.com/art/a-room-with-a-view/] You might find some other inspiring pictures in his collection.

6 Use a Bible Story

Imagine a Bible story unfolding with you standing on the side watching it. Perhaps you have seen the movie "The Christmas Carol". In it the ghosts of Christmas take Scrooge to view events in his life and in the life of others. He is standing on the side watching the event take place. Imagine yourself watching one of the Bible events take place.

One example is the baptism of Jesus (Matt. 3.13 – 17). In this story, God the Father, Son, and Holy Spirit are all present. The Father speaking, Jesus being baptized by John the Baptist, and the Holy Spirit in the form of a dove descending on Jesus.

You can use favorite Bible stories of your own, or you can read through the Gospels. One way to see the Gospels as stories is to use a harmony of the Gospels that puts the stories in one collection instead of four. One online harmony is http://so4j.com/harmony-of-the-gospels-of-jesus-in-the bible . This one uses hypertexts of references so it is possible to see text in pop-up windows. Another that puts the text in a screenplay format is www.bookofjesus.com/bojchron.htm. Another older one is A. T. Robertson's https://enduringword.com/ebooks/Harmony-of-the-Gospels-Robertson.pdf (Text begins on page 49 of this pdf document, after a lengthy index.)

How does God sending Christ the Messiah touch the story? How does Jesus' human experience as a Jewish man brought up in tradition, living in that time touch the story? Where do you see God's grace in our Savior? Where is the divinity, the Kingship of the Lord present? How do you see praise in the story? How are people in the story involved in praise, or how does the story bring praise from you? How does the story bring you into the presence of Jesus? (It is certainly possible that not all of these apply to each story that you would use.) What do you experience, to take with you, by meditating on a Bible story using these worship words?

For example, imagine being on the side at the wedding at Cana. (John 2) People have gathered for the celebration. Perhaps it is next to a building in a decorated courtyard. There are quite a few people. From John 1, there were at least 5 disciples, perhaps more. Perhaps the bride and groom are chatting and saying, "I didn't invite all these people." "Neither did I. But I heard mom inviting some and I bet your mother invited some we don't know about." Just then, the wine steward comes up to them and whispers something. You know he's talking about the wine being short. Somehow, Mary is passing by and hears. While the couple is looking like a disaster is coming at the beginning of their married life ("Yeah, I remember Simeon. He's the one who didn't have enough wine at his wedding..."), Mary goes over and talks to Jesus. He doesn't get up right away, but Mary goes off looking satisfied. [Christ: He was sent there at that moment. Jesus: He was a person, a person who got invited and enjoyed celebrations. Savior: He is a Person Who cares about people. Mary thinks that includes caring about people in physical needs. Apparently, Jesus does, too.]

Jesus gets up and walks over to the servants and talks to them. The servants look a little puzzled, but they start filling the six stone water pots with water. As you watch, one of the servants glances back at Jesus and sees Him smiling. You can see the servant, kind of surprised, glancing back again, but Jesus has moved away. [The Lord had stepped in and created blessing.] Then, one of the servants takes some of what was water for the steward to taste. The steward is surprised (probably because he thought the couple was going down the drain socially, not providing enough wine, and worrying about his tip). He tastes the wine and an impressed glow comes to his face. While he goes off (with a more respectful attitude) to talk to the couple, the servant who saw Jesus smile gets a look on his face like the sun just rose on a day so wonderful it is difficult to keep from dancing.

There are a lot of people who don't know what happened. However, the servants know, the disciples know, and the servant who saw Jesus smile has the beginning of praise and wonder bubbling up inside his heart. You can look ahead to the time when the news of Jesus' death and resurrection comes up to Cana and see this servant entering new life with his wife and children and spreading joy to others as well.

What do you take with you from this experience? Perhaps a new memory of Jesus' smile, a new appreciation of Jesus' caring, a new wonder at people who were changed forever by Jesus and who don't exactly get named in the Bible, and perhaps a stronger faith reaching out with the disciples whom you saw looking at Jesus in a sudden new way ("the first of His signs, and His disciples believed in Him."). Perhaps, you take more depth in your use of "Christ, Jesus, Savior, Lord, praise to You".

7 Further Study

This section is not meant to be a treatise of doctrine, but an overview of what the Lord has to say in His word in connection with these worship words.

Christ

There was Andrew, following John the Baptist. Can you imagine him coming home, crashing through the doorway, and shouting, breathlessly, "Simon, we have found the Messiah!" (John 1.40, 41) It's John who adds that, translated, this means "Christ".

It is Simon Peter who, later, makes it emphatic, "You are The Christ." (Matt.16.16)

There were some people who wanted to know who He was. The high priest (Matt. 26.63) and the chief priests and scribes among others (Luke 22.66, 67). Christ knew they would not believe Him if He told them. He did speak clearly and openly to the woman at the well when He said, "I who speak to you am He." (John 4.24-26) Aged Simeon knew Who Mary and Joseph were bringing in— it was the "Lord's Christ" (Luke 2.26) Paul opens the door to the past to show that the Rock that followed the Children of Israel in the desert was also, in fact, Christ. (1 Cor. 10.1-4)

There was another side to knowing Who He was. The demons that came out of people at the word of Christ knew very well Who He was. (Luke 4.41) Christ said there would be many other people who would come claiming to be the Christ. (Matt.24.5)

At the Day of Pentecost, Peter speaks to those the Spirit was bringing in and to the Church through the ages: "Therefore let all the house of Israel know for certain that God has made Him both Lord and Christ—this Jesus whom you crucified." (Acts 2.36)

What Christ says about Himself is that His Father sent Him. To see how much of a focus this is for Him, here are only the passages in John that refer to Christ being sent by the Father: John 4.34, 5.24, 5.30, 5.36-37, 6.38-39, 6.44, 6.57, 7.16, 7.28-29, 7.33, 8.16, 8.18, 8.26, 8.29, 8.42, 9.4, 11.42, 12.44-45, 12.49, 13.20, 14.24, 15.21, 16.5, 17.3, 17.8, 17.18, 17.21, 17.23, 17.25, and 20.21.

Then there are things that Christ did: He performed miracles (John 7.31), suffered (Luke 24.25-27), died (Rom 5.6), rose (Rom 6.4), opened people's minds to understand the Scriptures (Luke 24.45-47) and will reign forever (Rev. 11.15).

The writers of the New Testament write about our relationship to Christ. John describes his purpose in writing with these words, "but these have been written so that you may believe that Jesus is the Christ, the Son of God; and that believing you may have life in His name." (John 20.31)

Paul says we have died with Christ and will also live with Him. (Rom 6.8,9). He says Christ is in us. (Rom 8.9, 10) He says that faith comes by hearing the word of Christ (Rom 10.17). We are one body in Christ (Rom 12.4,5), we are crucified with Christ (Gal 2.20), we are clothed with Christ (Gal 3.27), for us, to live is Christ (Phil 1.21), we are raised up with Christ (Col 3.1), and John says that believing in Christ, we are born of God (1 John 5.1).

It is John who quotes Jesus, "This is eternal life, that they may know You, the only true God, and Jesus Christ whom You have sent." (John 17.3)

Jesus

Jesus has a genealogy that outshines any attempt today to trace ancestors. Matthew (1.1-16) and Luke (3.23-38) supply two sides of Jesus' family history.

In the Gospels of Matthew, Mark, and Luke, we see Jesus' birth. Mary His mother had been with child by the Holy Spirit. (Matt. 1.18) Jesus' name gives Him a mission, to "save His people from their sins." (Matt 1.21) Jesus grew up "increasing in wisdom and stature, and in favor with God and men." (Luke 2.52)

Jesus was baptized, the Holy Spirit descended on Him, and the Father said clearly, "You are My beloved Son, in You I am well-pleased." (Luke 3.21,22)

When Jesus began His ministry He was about 30. (Luke 3.23) He was led by the Holy Spirit to the desert to be tempted by the devil. (Luke 4.1,2) Jesus then returned in the power of the Holy Spirit (Luke 4.14) to preach, teach and heal. (Matt 4.17, 23) During His ministry, Jesus didn't have a permanent home and spent a lot of time living outdoors. (Matt 8.20) Along the way, He met a variety of people, including at least one whom He described as having great faith. (Luke 7.9)

His disciples experienced Jesus as very human, so tired He slept during a violent storm while they were at sea (Matt 8.24) and as divine when He woke to tell the wind and waves to go back to being calm (Luke 8.24). Jesus allowed power to come from Him to heal when someone touched Him (Luke 8.46), rebuked unclean spirits (Luke 9.42), and expected more of the ten lepers to return and say "Thank You" after they were healed. (Luke 17.17)

Jesus looked forward to children coming to Him (Luke 18.26), but refused to explain His authority to those who did not believe in

Him. (Luke 20.8) He knew what people were thinking without anyone telling Him. (Matt 9.4) He knew what was going to happen to Him and told His disciples ahead of time. (Mark 10.32) He gave His disciples authority to use over unclean spirits. (Matt 10.1) He withdrew from those who were conspiring against Him. (Matt 12.14-16)

When Jesus talked to people, He spoke in parables (Matt 13.34). He walked on the sea out to his disciples who were in a boat, and told them not to be afraid. (Matt 14.26, 27) He had compassion for the people He talked to, even to the point of feeding them. (Matt 15.32)

Jesus invited people to follow Him and told them it would be difficult (Matt 16.24). He took Peter, James, and John up a mountain and showed them His glory in great brightness while He talked with Moses and Elijah. (Matt 17.1-3)

Coming down the mountain, Jesus told His disciples He was going to be delivered into the hands of people who would kill Him, but that He would be raised from the dead. (Matt 17.22-23) Jesus showed anger at some of the activities in the temple, driving out those buying and selling. (Matt 21.12)

Before going to the cross, Jesus celebrated the Passover with His disciples. "While they were eating, Jesus took some bread, and after a blessing, He broke it and gave it to the disciples, and said, 'Take, eat; this is My body.' And when He had taken a cup and given thanks, He gave it to them, saying, 'Drink from it, all of you; for this is My blood of the covenant, which is poured out for many for forgiveness of sins.'" (Matt 26.26-28)

Jesus told Peter that He knew Peter was going to deny Him. (Matt 26.34) He took His disciples after the Passover meal to the

Garden of Gethsemane. (Matt 26.36) It was there that people came with swords and clubs to arrest Him. (Matt 26.50, 55)

Jesus kept silent before the High Priest, until finally telling him that he would see the Son of Man coming on the clouds of heaven. (Matt 26.62-64) Then, Jesus was scourged and crucified. (Matt 27.26) The charge put on Jesus' cross read, "This is Jesus the King of the Jews." (Matt 27.37)

Jesus said, "My God, My God, why have You forsaken Me?" (Matt. 27.46) and "Father into Your hands I commit my spirit." (Luke 23.46). Then, He gave up His spirit. (Matt 27.50) It was Joseph of Arimathea that took Jesus' body and wrapped it before putting it in the tomb. (Matt 27.57-59)

After He rose, Jesus met the women who came to prepare Him for final burial, letting them see Him and worship Him. (Matt 28.9) Before He ascended, Jesus appeared to the disciples and told them He had all authority, sending them to make disciples and to know He was with them always. (Matt 28.18-20)

In the Gospel of John, there are additional descriptions of Jesus: Grace and truth come through Jesus. (1.17) He is the Lamb of God who takes away the sin of the world. (1.29) He invited Philip to follow Him. (1.43) Philip witnessed to Nathaniel that Jesus is the One described in the Old Testament. (1.45)

Jesus' first miracle was turning water into wine in Cana. (2.11) He talked to the Samaritan woman at the well and offered living water. (4.9,10) Jesus told the woman that He was the Messiah promised (4.25,26). Jesus went on to heal a man's son (4.50) and tell people he is the bread of life. (6.35)

Jesus said His teaching came from the One Who sent Him. (7.16) He refused to condemn a woman who had sinned. (8.10-11) He said He is the Light of the world and gives people the Light of Life. (8.12) He boldly proclaimed "before Abraham was born, I am." (8.58) He told Martha "I am the resurrection and the life" (11.25, 26) He said (14.6) "I am the way, the truth, and the life."

Jesus said people who believed in Him were really believing in the One Who sent Him. (12.44) Jesus' kingdom was not of this world, He told people. (18.36) Then, in (19.18), John describes Jesus being crucified between two other men. From the cross He entrusted His mother to John (19.26, 27). He fulfilled Scripture by saying, "I am thirsty," and having received a drink, said, "It is finished" and gave up His spirit. (19.28, 30) His body was wrapped according to Jewish custom when it was taken from the cross. (19.40)

After His resurrection, Jesus spoke to Mary (20.14) and came to be with the disciples on Easter evening, giving them His peace and sending them out. (20.19, 21)

John says he wrote so that his readers might believe that Jesus is the Christ, thereby receiving eternal life. (20.30, 31)

In the remainder of the New Testament, Luke said God glorified Jesus (Acts 3.13) and Stephen saw Jesus at the right hand of God (Acts 7.55-56). The apostle Paul met Jesus (Acts 9.5). Peter testified that Jesus was anointed with the Holy Spirit and power (Acts 10.38).

Paul went on to write that the grace of God by Jesus, abounded to the many (Rom 5.15). Jesus is the foundation which has been laid (1 Cor 3.1). There is one Lord, Jesus, by whom are all things (1 Cor 8.6). Only by the Holy Spirit can one say that Jesus is Lord (1 Cor 12.3). Jesus is the cornerstone (Eph 2.19,20) and at His name every knee will bow and every tongue confess that Jesus is Lord (Phil 2.9-11).

Paul reminds the Thessalonians that they are waiting for Jesus to come from heaven, that He will rescue from the wrath to come (1 Thes 1.9,10), and that He is coming with all His saints (1 Thes 3.12,13). Paul reminds Timothy that Jesus is the one Mediator between God and man (1 Tim 2.5).

The writer of Hebrews says that Jesus was crowned with glory and honor, tasting death for everyone (Heb 2.9). He says Jesus is the forerunner for us and that He is Apostle and High Priest forever (Heb 3.1, 6.19,20). Jesus, he says, lives to make intercession for people (Heb 7.23-25).

The writer of Hebrews encourages us to fix our eyes on Jesus, "the author and perfecter of faith" (Heb 12.1,2) and the great Shepherd of the sheep. (Heb 13.20,21)

Peter remembers the transfiguration and says that He and James and John were eyewitnesses of Jesus' majesty. (2 Peter 1.16)

John writes of Jesus as the Advocate with the Father (1 John 2.1), as the Son of God (1 John 4.15) and as the Christ, born of God (1 John 5.1).

The New Testament ends with the Revelation of Jesus Christ (Rev. 1.1) and quotes Jesus saying, "I am the root and the descendant of David, the bright and morning star." (Rev 22.16)

Savior

Luke reports that there was a day when a Savior was born, and He "is Christ the Lord." (Luke 2.11)

After the woman at the well in Samaria witnessed to her neighbors, and after Jesus spent two days with the Samaritan people, they told the woman that they knew they had met the "Savior of the world." (John 4.42)

Luke in Acts says God exalted the Savior to His right hand to give repentance and forgiveness. (Acts 5.31) Later He says the Savior, Jesus, was a descendant of King David. (Acts 13.22, 23)

Paul says we are waiting for a Savior, and that He is the Lord Jesus Christ. (Phil 3.20) Paul reminds Timothy that God's grace has been revealed by the appearing of "our Savior Christ Jesus." (2 Tim 1.8-10) In writing to Titus, Paul says grace and peace come from our Savior. (Titus 1.4) And we look for the appearing of our Savior, who gave Himself to redeem us and purify us. (Titus 2.11-14)

Paul gives Titus and us a detailed description of God's actions through our Savior: "But when the kindness of God our Savior and His love for mankind appeared, He saved us, not on the basis of deeds which we have done in righteousness, but according to His mercy, by the washing of regeneration and renewing by the Holy Spirit, whom He poured out upon us richly through Jesus Christ our Savior." (Titus 3.4-6)

Peter says he writes to us, who have received faith by "the righteousness of our God and Savior, Jesus Christ." (2 Peter 1.1) John tells us that our Father has sent His Son "to be the Savior of the world." (1 John 4.14)

Lord

Is He Lord? Elizabeth recognized Mary as the mother of her Lord. (Luke 1.43) The One Luke reports being born in the city of David is "Christ the Lord." (Luke 2.11) Luke also quotes Isaiah that preparations are to be made for the way of the "Lord". (Luke 3.4) Simon Peter recognized his sinfulness in the presence of the Lord. (Luke 5.8) John the Baptist sent his disciples to the Lord. (Luke 7.19) The apostles asked the Lord to increase their faith. (Luke 17.5)

A leper wanting to be cleansed comes to the Lord. (Matt 8.2) A centurion comes to the Lord for his servant to be healed (Matt 8.8). The disciples appeal to the Lord to save them in a storm. (Matt 8.25) A blind man believes the Lord can heal him (Matt 9.28) A Canaanite woman begs for mercy from the Lord for her daughter. (Matt 15.22) A father begs for mercy for his son. (Matt 17.15) Zacchaeus promises the Lord that he will change his life. (Luke 19.8)

The message the disciples are given to allow them to use someone's donkey is "The Lord has need of them." (Matt 21.3) Jesus says to the Pharisees that the Messiah, Christ, the son of David, was called Lord by David. (Matt 22.42-44) Peter addresses the Lord when he says he is willing to die with Him. (Luke 22.33) The women on Easter did not find the body of the Lord. (Luke 24.3) The Emmaus disciples witnessed that the Lord had risen. (Luke 24.33-34)

Looking at the Gospel of John, Peter says the Lord has the words of eternal life. (6.68) The Lord does not condemn the woman caught in adultery (8.11) A man the Lord healed from blindness told Him, "Lord I believe." Then he worshiped the Lord. (9.38) Martha said, "Yes, Lord, I have believed that You are the Christ, the Son of God, even He who comes into the world." (11.27)

Simon Peter was amazed that the Lord wanted to wash his feet. (13.6) The Lord said it was right to call Him, "Lord." (13.13) Mary Magdalene told the disciples that she had seen the Lord. (20.18) On Easter evening, the disciples "rejoiced when they saw the Lord." (20.20) A week later, Thomas confessed, "My Lord and my God!" (20.28)

Luke, in Acts, reports that the disciples coming together after Easter were asking the Lord if it were time for the kingdom to be restored. (1.6) In Peter's sermon he says, "God has made Him both Lord and Christ…" (2.36) Ananias told Saul it was the Lord Jesus Who sent him. (9.17) After that, Saul went around and spoke boldly "in the name of the Lord." (9.28) After Saul performed miracles "many believed in the Lord." (9.41-42) Peter told Cornelius and his friends (with amazement) that Jesus is "Lord of all". (10.36) Peter told the assembled group of disciples in Jerusalem "I remembered the word of the Lord" to justify his actions. (11.16) He went on saying "we believe that we are saved through the grace of the Lord Jesus." (15.11) In Philippi, Paul told the jailer and his family, "believe in the Lord Jesus, and you will be saved…" (16.31) Another one to believe in the Lord was Crispus. (18.8) Paul says that he received his ministry from the Lord Jesus (20.24) Before Paul was arrested, "the Lord stood at his side and said, 'Take courage…'" (23.11)

In Paul's letters he refers to the Lord: "For the wages of sin is death, but the free gift of God is eternal life in Christ Jesus our Lord." (Rom 6.23) He told the Romans to confess with their mouths Jesus as Lord. (Rom 10.9) He told them to put on the Lord Jesus Christ. (Rom 13.14) He said we live or die for the Lord. (Rom 14.8) The purpose of Christ dying and living again, Paul says, is that "He might be Lord both of the dead and of the living." (Rom 14.9)

Paul told the Corinthians that we wait eagerly for the revelation of our Lord. (1 Cor 1.7) He wanted the people there to have undistracted devotion to the Lord. (1 Cor 7.35) He told them there is one Lord, "by whom are all things." (1 Cor 8.6)

Paul describes the night before the Lord died: "For I received from the Lord that which I also delivered to you, that the Lord Jesus in the night in which He was betrayed took bread; and when He had given thanks, He broke it and said, 'This is My body, which is for you; do this in remembrance of Me.' In the same way He took the cup also after supper, saying, 'This cup is the new covenant in My blood; do this, as often as you drink it, in remembrance of Me.' For as often as you eat this bread and drink the cup, you proclaim the Lord's death until He comes." (1 Cor 11.23-26)

It is only by the Holy Spirit that a person can say, "Jesus is Lord." (1 Cor 12.3) God gives us the victory through our Lord. (1 Cor 15.57) Paul says he preaches Christ Jesus as Lord. (2 Cor 4.5) He says he is looking forward to being at home with the Lord. (2 Cor 5.8) Paul was impressed with the Macedonian Christians because in their financial giving, they first gave themselves to the Lord. (2 Cor 8.5)

Paul says there is a time coming when every person will confess that Jesus Christ is Lord. (Phil 2.9-11) He says nothing is of more value than knowing Christ Jesus his Lord. (Phil 3.8) He encourages the Colossians to walk in the Lord. (Col 2.6,7) He prays that the Lord will cause the Thessalonian Christians to increase in love for one another. (1 Thes 3.12,13) At the end, the Lord will descend from heaven and Christians will meet the Lord in the air. (1 Thes 4.16, 17) Paul tells Timothy, "I thank Christ Jesus our Lord, who has strengthened me, because He considered me faithful, putting me into service" (1 Tim 1.12)

James says the coming of the Lord is near. (James 5.8) Peter says he was an eyewitness of the Lord's majesty. (2 Peter 1.16) In Revelations, the Lord says that He is the Alpha and the Omega, "who is and who was and who is to come, the Almighty." (Rev 1.7,8) As John finishes Revelations, he says, "Come, Lord Jesus." (Rev 22.20)

Praise

These references refer to praise given to God.

King David appointed some of the Levites serving at the tabernacle to the ministry of praising the Lord. (1 Chron 16.4) When the people heard a psalm read, they praised the Lord (1 Chron 16.36). In the Psalms there are frequent invitations to praise the Lord and encouragements that praise is "becoming to the upright". (Psalms 9.11, 22.23, 33.1, 34.1, 102.18, 104.33, 113.3, 147.1)

In particular, David writes in Psalm 51.15: "O Lord, open my lips, that my mouth may declare Your praise."

Isaiah encourages praising the Lord in song as a way of letting people know what excellent things the Lord has done. (Is. 12.5)

When Jesus was born, the angels praised God. (Luke 2.13,14) The shepherds, too, praised God (Luke 2.20). As Jesus came into Jerusalem, the crowd of disciples praised God. (Luke 19.37) The early church gathered daily and praised God. (Acts 2.46, 47) Paul quotes Isaiah "Praise the Lord all you Gentiles." (Rom 15.11)

One particular passage shows people praising Jesus: "And He began teaching in their synagogues and was praised by all." (Luke 4.15) Thayer's Greek Lexicon gives this meaning to the word Luke used in that passage (and its other uses in the New Testament): "to praise, extol, magnify, celebrate; to honor, do honor to, hold in honor; to make glorious, adorn with lustre, clothe with splendor; to impart glory to something, render it excellent; to make renowned, render illustrious, i.e. to cause the dignity and worth of some person or thing to become manifest and acknowledged." [http://biblehub.com/Greek/1392.htm]

To

These references are to personal involvement in praise.

In Exodus 15.2: "This is my God, and I will praise him." "I will sing praise to the Lord." (Judges 5.3) "I will sing praises to your name." (2 Sam 22.50, Ps 18.49)

Jesus also gave this example: "At that time Jesus said, 'I praise You, Father...'" (Matt 11.25, Luke 10.21)

Encouragement for our personal involvement is in Rev 19.5: "And a voice came from the throne, saying, 'Give praise to our God, all you His bond-servants, you who fear Him, the small and the great.'"

You

These references give assurance that the Lord is here to receive our praise:

Jesus gave encouragement to the disciples, when He said, "I am with you always." (Matt 28.19, 20) Then Jesus speaks these words in John 14.16, 17: "I will ask the Father, and He will give you another Helper, that He may be with you forever; that is the Spirit of truth, whom the world cannot receive, because it does not see Him or know Him, but you know Him because He abides with you and will be in you."

Jesus goes on to say, "In that day you will know that I am in My Father, and you in Me, and I in you." (John 14.20) And again in that chapter He says, "If anyone loves Me, he will keep My word; and My Father will love him, and We will come to him and make Our abode with him." (John 14.23)

These passages give examples of people praising God personally:

"I will give thanks to You, O Lord." (2 Sam 22.50)

"I will sing praise to Your name." (Ps 9.2)

"I love You, O Lord, my strength." (Ps 18.1)

"You have turned for me my mourning into dancing;
You have loosed my sackcloth and girded me with gladness,
That my soul may sing praise to You and not be silent.
O Lord my God, I will give thanks to You forever." (Ps 30.11-12)

"Because Your lovingkindness is better than life,
My lips will praise You." (Ps 63.3)

"I will sing of lovingkindness and justice,
To You, O Lord, I will sing praises." (Ps 101.1)

"Seven times a day I praise You,
Because of Your righteous ordinances." (Ps 119.164)

"I will sing a new song to You, O God;
Upon a harp of ten strings I will sing praises to You" (Ps 144.9)

"Every day I will bless You,
And I will praise Your name forever and ever." (Ps 145.2)

Epilogue

Thank you for reading this booklet. I pray that our Father and the Spirit and the One Who is Christ, Jesus, Savior, Lord will bless you in close daily walking with Him, praising Him, talking with Him, and listening to Him in Life now and forever, and that you will be a blessing in leading others to Him.

Christ, Jesus, Savior, Lord, praise to You!

Printed in Great Britain
by Amazon

26398222R00036